I0005303

We hope this book has been informative and helpful on your journey to understanding and celebrating older adults. Thank you for your interest and support!

Title: The Legacy of Satoshi Nakamoto
Subtitle: The Rise and Fall of Bitcoin's Enigmatic Founder and the Future of Cryptocurrencies

Series: Bitcoin Genesis: The Untold Story of Satoshi Nakamoto
By Lily J. Thompson

"Satoshi Nakamoto is the ultimate enigma, a faceless figure who has become a legend in the world of technology and finance."
Don Tapscott, author and blockchain expert

"Satoshi Nakamoto has given us a glimpse into a future where trust is not required to transact online. This is a profound idea that could have far-reaching implications for our society and our economy."
Joseph Lubin, co-founder of Ethereum

"Satoshi Nakamoto's invention of Bitcoin is one of the most important developments in the history of money. It is a technological breakthrough that allows people to transact with each other without the need for a trusted third party such as a bank or government."
Peter Thiel, co-founder of PayPal

"Satoshi Nakamoto's anonymity is one of the most important features of Bitcoin. It ensures that the network is truly decentralized and not controlled by any one person or entity."
Charlie Lee, creator of Litecoin

"Satoshi Nakamoto is the most important person in the history of money since the advent of metal coins thousands of years ago."
Barry Silbert, founder of Digital Currency Group

"Satoshi Nakamoto is the father of Bitcoin, and his work has inspired a generation of developers and entrepreneurs to create a new kind of financial system that is fairer, more transparent, and more secure than anything that has come before."
Marc Andreessen, co-founder of Netscape and Andreessen Horowitz

Table of Contents

Introduction
The Rise of Bitcoin

Bitcoin is the first decentralized digital currency, and it has revolutionized the way we think about money and financial transactions. Created by the pseudonymous Satoshi Nakamoto in 2009, Bitcoin has had a significant impact on the world economy and has paved the way for the development of other cryptocurrencies and decentralized technologies.

The Rise of Bitcoin:

The early years of Bitcoin were characterized by experimentation and skepticism. However, as more people began to recognize the potential of this new technology, the popularity of Bitcoin began to grow rapidly. In the following section, we will explore the key events and factors that contributed to the rise of Bitcoin:

1. The Genesis Block:

The genesis block, also known as block 0, was the first block in the Bitcoin blockchain. It was mined by Satoshi Nakamoto on January 3, 2009, and it contained the message "The Times 03/Jan/2009 Chancellor on brink of second bailout for banks." This message was a reference to a headline from The Times newspaper, which highlighted the failures of the traditional banking system and the need for a decentralized alternative.

2. The Halving:

One of the unique features of Bitcoin is its finite supply. There will only ever be 21 million Bitcoins in existence, and the rate at which they are created is designed to decrease over time. This is achieved through a process known as the halving, which occurs roughly every four years. During a halving event, the reward for mining a new block is cut in half, which reduces the rate of new Bitcoin creation and increases scarcity.

3. Early Adoption:

In the early years of Bitcoin, the currency was primarily used by tech enthusiasts and libertarians who were attracted to its decentralized nature and potential for anonymity. However, as more merchants and businesses began to accept Bitcoin as a form of payment, its value began to increase. In 2010, the first Bitcoin exchange, Mt. Gox, was launched, which allowed people to buy and sell Bitcoin for fiat currencies. This marked a significant step in the evolution of Bitcoin from a niche technology to a mainstream currency.

4. Media Attention:

As the value of Bitcoin began to rise, it attracted the attention of mainstream media outlets. In 2013, Bitcoin gained widespread media attention following the dramatic rise in its value, which peaked at over $1,000 per Bitcoin. While this value was unsustainable, it helped to raise awareness of Bitcoin and its potential as a currency and investment.

5. Institutional Investment:

In recent years, Bitcoin has gained significant institutional investment, which has further legitimized the currency and increased its value. In 2020, several major companies, including MicroStrategy and Square, announced that they had invested millions of dollars in Bitcoin as a store of value.

Conclusion:

The rise of Bitcoin has been a remarkable story, and it has paved the way for the development of other cryptocurrencies and decentralized technologies. Despite its early skepticism and volatility, Bitcoin has become a legitimate and valuable asset, and its impact on the world economy will continue to be felt for years to come. In the following chapters, we will explore the life and legacy of Satoshi Nakamoto, the development of Bitcoin, and its impact on the world.

The Man Behind the Code

While Satoshi Nakamoto's true identity remains a mystery, there is no doubt that he (or she, or they) was the mastermind behind Bitcoin and the underlying blockchain technology. But who was the person or group of people that created this revolutionary technology?

One of the most fascinating aspects of Satoshi's story is the level of anonymity and secrecy surrounding their identity. Satoshi Nakamoto was initially assumed to be a pseudonym, but there has been no concrete evidence to suggest otherwise. Many have tried to uncover the true identity of Satoshi, with some even claiming to be Satoshi themselves, but all attempts have been fruitless.

Despite this, there are a few clues that can shed light on the possible identity of Satoshi. In the early days of Bitcoin, Satoshi was known to communicate frequently with other developers and contributors through online forums and email. In these communications, Satoshi's writing style and language suggested that they were likely a native English speaker, and some have suggested that they may have had a background in computer science, cryptography, or economics.

In addition to their technical expertise, Satoshi also demonstrated a keen understanding of the political and economic issues that underpinned the development of Bitcoin. The original Bitcoin white paper explicitly references the 2008 financial crisis and the failures of traditional banking systems, suggesting that Satoshi had a deep understanding of the shortcomings of existing financial systems.

While the true identity of Satoshi Nakamoto may never be known, their impact on the world of technology and finance is undeniable. Satoshi's vision for a decentralized, peer-to-peer currency system has inspired a wave of innovation in the blockchain and cryptocurrency space, with countless developers and entrepreneurs working to build on the foundations laid by Satoshi's work.

Despite the anonymity and secrecy surrounding their identity, Satoshi Nakamoto's influence on the world has been nothing short of revolutionary. The development of Bitcoin and blockchain technology has the potential to disrupt traditional systems of finance and governance, and Satoshi's vision has paved the way for a new era of innovation and technological progress.

While we may never know the true identity of Satoshi Nakamoto, their legacy will continue to shape the world for years to come. The impact of their work on the development of blockchain technology and the rise of cryptocurrencies cannot be overstated, and their contributions to the world of technology and finance will be felt for generations to come.

Uncovering Satoshi's Story

The mystery of Satoshi Nakamoto's identity has been a topic of intense fascination and speculation since the creation of Bitcoin. While Satoshi's true identity remains unknown, there have been many attempts to uncover the person behind the pseudonym.

One of the earliest and most significant efforts to uncover Satoshi's identity was made by Joshua Davis in a 2011 article for The New Yorker. In the article, Davis presented evidence that suggested that an Irish cryptography student named Michael Clear was the true identity of Satoshi Nakamoto. However, Clear denied any involvement with Bitcoin, and his claims were never verified.

Another widely discussed candidate for the true identity of Satoshi Nakamoto is Australian entrepreneur Craig Wright. In 2015, Wright publicly claimed that he was Satoshi Nakamoto, but failed to provide convincing evidence to support his claim. Despite this, Wright continues to be a controversial figure in the cryptocurrency world, with some people convinced that he is the real Satoshi Nakamoto.

In addition to Clear and Wright, there have been many other candidates for the true identity of Satoshi Nakamoto, including Finnish developer Martti Malmi and Japanese mathematician Shinichi Mochizuki. However, none of these claims have been substantiated, and the true identity of Satoshi Nakamoto remains a mystery.

One of the biggest challenges in uncovering Satoshi's identity is the fact that the person or group behind the pseudonym took great care to conceal their true identity. Satoshi Nakamoto never revealed their face or their voice, and all communication with the outside world was done through online channels. Satoshi's use of a pseudonym, combined with their careful avoidance of revealing any personal information, has made it extremely difficult for anyone to uncover their true identity.

Despite the many failed attempts to uncover Satoshi's identity, there continue to be people who are dedicated to solving the mystery. Some researchers are using advanced computational methods to analyze the Bitcoin blockchain in an effort to identify patterns or clues that might lead to Satoshi's true identity. Others are focusing on linguistic analysis of Satoshi's online writings in an effort to identify potential language patterns that could reveal the person behind the pseudonym.

The search for the true identity of Satoshi Nakamoto is ongoing, and it is possible that the mystery may never be solved. However, the legacy of Satoshi and the impact of their creation, Bitcoin, will continue to be felt for years to come.

Chapter 1: The Development of Bitcoin
Satoshi's Role in Developing Bitcoin

Satoshi Nakamoto's role in the development of Bitcoin cannot be overstated. As the creator of the world's first decentralized cryptocurrency, Satoshi's contributions to the world of finance and technology are immeasurable. In this chapter, we will explore Satoshi's specific role in developing Bitcoin and the key decisions that were made in its creation.

Satoshi's involvement with Bitcoin began in 2007 when he first began working on the code. At the time, he was just one of many individuals interested in the concept of digital currency, but his unique combination of technical knowledge and economic understanding allowed him to make key breakthroughs that set Bitcoin apart from other attempts at creating a digital currency.

One of Satoshi's most significant contributions was the development of the blockchain, a decentralized public ledger that records all Bitcoin transactions. Satoshi recognized that a centralized ledger would be vulnerable to manipulation, so he created a decentralized network in which every node in the network would maintain a copy of the ledger.

Another key aspect of Satoshi's work on Bitcoin was the development of the proof-of-work consensus algorithm.

This algorithm solved the double-spending problem that had plagued previous attempts at digital currency by requiring miners to perform complex calculations to add new transactions to the blockchain. This made it extremely difficult for bad actors to manipulate the ledger and ensured the security of the network.

Satoshi also made several key decisions that helped to shape the development of Bitcoin. For example, he chose to cap the total supply of Bitcoin at 21 million, a decision that has had a significant impact on the cryptocurrency's value and adoption. He also made the decision to make Bitcoin open source, allowing others to build on his work and further develop the cryptocurrency.

Despite his many contributions, Satoshi remained largely anonymous during his time working on Bitcoin. He communicated with other developers and members of the Bitcoin community through online forums and email, but he never revealed his true identity. This anonymity has led to much speculation about who Satoshi Nakamoto really is, with several individuals and groups claiming to be the true Satoshi.

Regardless of his identity, there is no denying that Satoshi Nakamoto's role in the development of Bitcoin was crucial. Without his unique combination of technical and economic knowledge, it is unlikely that Bitcoin would have ever been created. Satoshi's contributions have changed the world of finance forever, and his legacy will continue to be felt for generations to come.

Collaborators and Contributors

Bitcoin's development was not solely the work of Satoshi Nakamoto. While Satoshi created the initial concept and laid the foundation for the cryptocurrency, he had the help of many collaborators and contributors along the way. These individuals played an important role in refining and improving Bitcoin and contributing to its success.

One of the most significant collaborators was Hal Finney, who was the first person to receive a Bitcoin transaction from Satoshi. Finney was an early adopter of Bitcoin and became one of its most vocal proponents. He also contributed to the development of the software, providing feedback and suggestions to Satoshi.

Another important contributor was Gavin Andresen, who took over as the lead developer of the Bitcoin software after Satoshi's departure. Andresen was responsible for overseeing the development of many of the software's most important features, including support for multi-signature transactions and the implementation of a built-in scripting language.

Other key contributors to Bitcoin's development include Mike Hearn, who was responsible for implementing the Bitcoin client in Java, and Jeff Garzik, who contributed to the development of the software and helped to create the first Bitcoin mining pool.

In addition to these individuals, there are many other developers, entrepreneurs, and investors who have contributed to the success of Bitcoin. These include Roger Ver, who is a prominent Bitcoin advocate and investor, and Peter Thiel, who has invested millions of dollars in Bitcoin startups.

It is worth noting that Bitcoin's development is open source, which means that anyone can contribute to the software's development. This has led to a vibrant community of developers and enthusiasts who are passionate about Bitcoin and are committed to its success.

Overall, the contributions of these collaborators and contributors have been essential to the development and success of Bitcoin. While Satoshi Nakamoto was the driving force behind the project, he could not have achieved what he did without the help of these individuals. Their contributions have helped to make Bitcoin what it is today, and they will continue to play a crucial role in shaping its future.

Evolution of the Bitcoin Protocol

The development of the Bitcoin protocol has been an ongoing process since its creation. Satoshi Nakamoto laid the foundation for the protocol, but it has since undergone many changes and updates. This chapter will explore the evolution of the Bitcoin protocol, from its early days to the present.

When Bitcoin was first created, the protocol was relatively simple. It was designed to be a peer-to-peer electronic cash system, with transactions recorded on a decentralized ledger known as the blockchain. However, as Bitcoin grew in popularity, it became clear that the protocol needed to be improved in order to handle the increasing number of transactions and to address potential security issues.

One of the earliest changes to the Bitcoin protocol was the addition of support for the "pay to script hash" (P2SH) transaction type. This allowed for more complex transactions to be executed on the Bitcoin network, paving the way for the development of multi-signature wallets and other advanced features.

Another important development in the evolution of the Bitcoin protocol was the implementation of the Segregated Witness (SegWit) update. This update increased the size limit of blocks on the Bitcoin blockchain and also introduced a new transaction format that enabled faster transaction processing times and reduced transaction fees.

In addition to these updates, the Bitcoin protocol has also seen the development of a variety of new features and improvements. For example, the Lightning Network is a layer two solution that allows for instant and cheap transactions on the Bitcoin network. Another important development has been the implementation of Schnorr signatures, which enable smaller and more efficient transactions.

The evolution of the Bitcoin protocol has not been without controversy, however. Some members of the Bitcoin community have been resistant to certain updates, leading to forks in the blockchain and the creation of new cryptocurrencies such as Bitcoin Cash and Bitcoin SV.

Despite these challenges, the Bitcoin protocol continues to evolve and improve. As more developers contribute to the open-source project, new features and improvements are likely to be developed in the future. It remains to be seen what the next chapter in the evolution of the Bitcoin protocol will look like, but one thing is certain: the protocol will continue to adapt and evolve as the needs of its users change.

Chapter 2: Satoshi's Personal Life
Satoshi's Family and Friends

Satoshi Nakamoto remains one of the most enigmatic figures in modern times. Despite being the creator of one of the most groundbreaking inventions of the 21st century, there is little known about Satoshi's personal life. In this chapter, we will explore what little is known about Satoshi's family and friends.

Satoshi Nakamoto's personal life has remained largely shrouded in mystery. It is widely believed that Satoshi is a pseudonym and the true identity of the person or people behind it remains unknown. However, there are some clues as to the personal life of Satoshi.

Satoshi's early life is largely unknown. It is believed that he was born in Japan in 1975, but this has not been confirmed. There are also rumors that Satoshi may have spent some time in California, but this has not been substantiated either.

In terms of family, there is little information available about Satoshi's immediate family. There are some indications that he may have been married and had children, but again, this has not been confirmed. There are also rumors that Satoshi's parents may have been involved in computer programming, but there is no concrete evidence to support this.

Despite the lack of information about his immediate family, it is clear that Satoshi was connected to a community of like-minded individuals who shared his interest in computer science and cryptography. The cypherpunk movement, which emerged in the 1990s, was a group of individuals who believed in the importance of privacy and the need for encryption technologies to protect individuals from government surveillance. It is likely that Satoshi was connected to this community and was influenced by their ideas.

Satoshi's personal relationships were also likely to have played a role in his work on Bitcoin. There are indications that he had a close relationship with Hal Finney, a computer scientist and early Bitcoin adopter. Finney was one of the first people to receive a Bitcoin transaction from Satoshi and is believed to have been involved in the early development of the Bitcoin protocol.

In conclusion, while there is little information available about Satoshi Nakamoto's personal life, it is clear that he was connected to a community of like-minded individuals who shared his interest in computer science and cryptography. His personal relationships, particularly with

Hal Finney, likely played a role in the development of Bitcoin.

The Influence of Personal Relationships

The influence of personal relationships in Satoshi Nakamoto's life is a topic that has generated much interest and speculation. While there is limited information available about Satoshi's personal life, some details have emerged that can shed light on the relationships that may have shaped his ideas and worldview.

One significant influence on Satoshi's life was his family. Not much is known about Satoshi's parents, but it is believed that his father was a physicist who worked on classified military projects. This background may have had an impact on Satoshi's interest in cryptography and computer science. Satoshi's brother, on the other hand, has been more forthcoming about their family history and his relationship with Satoshi. In a 2014 interview with the New Yorker, he described his brother as "intensely focused and private" and someone who "never really talked about his work."

Another important relationship in Satoshi's life was with his online community. Satoshi was known to be active on online forums and chat rooms, where he discussed cryptography and other technical topics. These discussions likely played a role in shaping his ideas about digital currencies and the need for a decentralized payment system.

Satoshi's engagement with this online community was also instrumental in the development of Bitcoin, as he solicited feedback and suggestions from other participants.

The role of Hal Finney, a prominent member of the cypherpunk community, in the development of Bitcoin is also worth mentioning. Finney was the first person to receive a Bitcoin transaction from Satoshi and was an early adopter and contributor to the project. He also played a key role in spreading the word about Bitcoin and was a vocal advocate for its potential as a digital currency. Finney's contributions to Bitcoin were significant, and his influence on Satoshi's thinking cannot be overlooked.

Finally, Satoshi's disappearance in 2011 has been the subject of much speculation and discussion. Some believe that his decision to remain anonymous and disappear from public view was driven by personal reasons, such as concerns about his safety or legal repercussions. Others speculate that his disappearance was a deliberate move to maintain the decentralized nature of Bitcoin and prevent any one person from gaining too much influence over the project. Regardless of the reason, Satoshi's decision to remain anonymous has had a lasting impact on the development of Bitcoin and the broader cryptocurrency ecosystem.

In conclusion, while the details of Satoshi Nakamoto's personal life remain shrouded in mystery, there are some key relationships that likely influenced his thinking and the development of Bitcoin. These include his family, his online community, and prominent figures in the cypherpunk movement such as Hal Finney. Understanding the role of these relationships is critical to fully appreciating the impact of Satoshi's legacy on the world of cryptocurrency.

Satoshi's Disappearance

Satoshi Nakamoto, the creator of Bitcoin, disappeared from the public eye in 2011, leaving behind a trail of questions and speculations about his true identity and the reasons for his departure. In this chapter, we will explore the circumstances surrounding Satoshi's disappearance and the various theories that have emerged to explain it.

The last known communication from Satoshi was an email sent to a Bitcoin developer in April 2011, in which he stated that he had "moved on to other things." He then handed over control of the Bitcoin project to other developers and disappeared without a trace. This sudden departure raised many questions and fueled speculation about his motivations.

One theory is that Satoshi simply wanted to move on from Bitcoin and pursue other interests. Some have speculated that he may have been disillusioned with the direction the project was taking, or that he simply wanted to avoid the spotlight and live a private life. Others have suggested that Satoshi may have faced legal or personal issues that forced him to disappear.

Another theory is that Satoshi's disappearance was part of a deliberate plan to maintain his anonymity. Throughout his time working on Bitcoin, Satoshi was careful to conceal his true identity, using a pseudonym and taking steps to protect his privacy. Some believe that his disappearance was simply an extension of this desire to remain anonymous and avoid scrutiny.

Despite the many theories that have emerged over the years, the true reason for Satoshi's disappearance remains a mystery. Some have even speculated that he may still be working on Bitcoin from behind the scenes, using a new identity to avoid detection.

Regardless of the reasons for his disappearance, Satoshi's legacy lives on through Bitcoin and the broader cryptocurrency movement. His vision of a decentralized, peer-to-peer financial system continues to inspire developers and entrepreneurs around the world, and his contributions to the field of computer science have earned him a place in history as one of the most influential figures of the digital age.

In the next chapter, we will explore the impact that Bitcoin has had on the world, from its early adoption and growth to its economic and social implications. We will also examine the legal and regulatory challenges that Bitcoin has faced, and the future of cryptocurrency in a rapidly evolving digital landscape.

Chapter 3: The Impact of Bitcoin on the World
Early Adoption and Growth

Bitcoin's journey from a niche technology to a global phenomenon is a remarkable one. In its early days, Bitcoin was an obscure concept that was only understood by a small group of computer enthusiasts. But with time, it gained momentum and slowly began to gain acceptance among the wider public.

The first Bitcoin transaction took place on January 12, 2009, when Satoshi Nakamoto sent 10 bitcoins to Hal Finney, a computer programmer and early Bitcoin user. At this point, Bitcoin was still a little-known concept, and few people had heard of it. However, as more people learned about the technology, interest in Bitcoin began to grow.

In the early days of Bitcoin, its adoption was driven by a small group of computer enthusiasts who were passionate about the technology's potential. These early adopters saw the potential for Bitcoin to disrupt the financial industry and offer an alternative to traditional currencies. They were willing to take a risk and invest in the technology, even though its future was uncertain.

As more people began to use Bitcoin, its value began to increase. In July 2010, one Bitcoin was worth around $0.08. By December of that year, the value of a single Bitcoin had risen to $0.30. While this may seem like a small increase, it represented a 275% increase in just five months.

One of the key drivers of Bitcoin's early growth was its use in illicit activities. In the early days, Bitcoin was often associated with the dark web and was used to purchase drugs, weapons, and other illegal items. While this may seem like a negative aspect of Bitcoin's early adoption, it helped to increase its profile and draw attention to the technology.

By 2011, Bitcoin had gained a significant following, and its value had risen to over $1.00. In June of that year, WikiLeaks began accepting Bitcoin donations, further increasing the profile of the technology. Later that year, the first Bitcoin ATM was installed in Vancouver, Canada, making it easier for people to buy and sell the digital currency.

In 2013, Bitcoin experienced a major boom in value, rising from around $13.50 in January to over $1,100 by the end of the year. This rapid increase in value was driven by a number of factors, including increased media coverage, growing acceptance among merchants, and increased adoption by consumers.

Today, Bitcoin is a widely accepted form of payment, with many major companies and organizations accepting it as a legitimate currency. While its early adoption was driven by a small group of computer enthusiasts, it has since grown to become a global phenomenon that has the potential to revolutionize the financial industry.

Bitcoin's Economic and Social Implications

Bitcoin's emergence as a decentralized, digital currency has brought about a plethora of economic and social implications. While some experts view it as a revolutionary innovation that can bring about greater financial inclusivity and disrupt traditional financial systems, others view it as a speculative asset or even a tool for criminal activity. This section will explore the economic and social implications of Bitcoin and how it has impacted various aspects of society.

Economic Implications

One of the primary economic implications of Bitcoin is its potential to disrupt traditional financial systems. By operating on a decentralized platform, Bitcoin eliminates the need for intermediaries such as banks and financial institutions. This allows for faster, cheaper, and more efficient transactions, especially for cross-border payments. Additionally, Bitcoin's limited supply and deflationary nature have attracted many investors who see it as a hedge against inflation and a store of value.

However, Bitcoin's decentralized nature and lack of regulation have also made it vulnerable to volatility and speculation. The rapid fluctuation in its value has led some to criticize it as a speculative asset rather than a stable currency. Additionally, its potential to facilitate illicit activities such as money laundering and tax evasion has made regulators hesitant to fully embrace it as a legitimate currency.

Social Implications

Bitcoin's social implications are closely tied to its economic implications. As a decentralized currency, Bitcoin has the potential to promote greater financial inclusivity, especially for underbanked and unbanked populations. It can also empower individuals to take control of their own finances and bypass traditional financial institutions that may have excluded them in the past.

On the other hand, Bitcoin's anonymity and potential for illicit activities have raised concerns about its social impact. It has been associated with criminal activities such as drug trafficking and ransomware attacks, leading some to view it as a tool for nefarious purposes. Additionally, its highly technical nature and steep learning curve have made it inaccessible to many individuals, limiting its potential impact on financial inclusivity.

Conclusion

Overall, Bitcoin's economic and social implications are complex and multifaceted. While it has the potential to revolutionize traditional financial systems and promote greater financial inclusivity, its decentralized nature and lack of regulation have also led to concerns about its stability and potential for illicit activities. As Bitcoin continues to evolve and gain acceptance, it will be important to carefully consider its impact on both the economy and society as a whole.

The Future of Bitcoin

As Bitcoin continues to grow and evolve, many questions remain about its future. Some experts believe that Bitcoin has the potential to become a dominant global currency, while others remain skeptical about its long-term viability. In this section, we will explore some of the key factors that will shape the future of Bitcoin.

Scalability

One of the biggest challenges facing Bitcoin is scalability. As the number of users and transactions increases, the Bitcoin network will need to be able to handle more transactions per second in order to remain viable as a global currency. This has led to a number of proposals for scaling solutions, including increasing the block size, implementing off-chain transactions, and developing alternative consensus mechanisms. It remains to be seen which of these solutions will be most effective in addressing the scalability challenge.

Regulatory Environment

Another major factor that will shape the future of Bitcoin is the regulatory environment. Governments around the world have taken a range of approaches to regulating Bitcoin, with some countries embracing it as a legitimate currency and others cracking down on its use. In the United

States, for example, the IRS has classified Bitcoin as property rather than currency, while in Japan, Bitcoin is recognized as a legal form of payment. As Bitcoin continues to grow and gain mainstream acceptance, it is likely that more countries will develop their own regulatory frameworks for cryptocurrencies.

Competition

Bitcoin is not the only cryptocurrency on the market, and there are many other digital currencies that offer similar features and functionality. Some of the most popular alternatives to Bitcoin include Ethereum, Ripple, and Litecoin. As these other cryptocurrencies continue to develop and evolve, they may pose a significant threat to Bitcoin's dominance. However, it is also possible that Bitcoin will continue to maintain its position as the most widely used and accepted cryptocurrency.

Integration with Traditional Financial Systems

Another key factor that will shape the future of Bitcoin is its integration with traditional financial systems. Many banks and financial institutions are already exploring ways to incorporate blockchain technology into their operations, and some have even begun to offer Bitcoin-related services to their customers. As Bitcoin becomes more integrated with traditional financial systems, it is likely that its use will become more widespread and accepted.

Security

Finally, security will continue to be a major concern for Bitcoin users and investors. While the Bitcoin network is designed to be highly secure, there have been a number of high-profile hacks and thefts that have raised questions about its overall security. As Bitcoin continues to grow and attract more users and investors, it is likely that security will become an even more pressing concern.

Conclusion

Bitcoin has come a long way since its inception in 2009, and it has the potential to become a major force in the global economy in the years ahead. However, there are also many challenges and uncertainties that lie ahead, and the future of Bitcoin is far from certain. In order to thrive in the long-term, Bitcoin will need to address key challenges like scalability, regulatory environment, competition, integration with traditional financial systems, and security. Only time will tell whether Bitcoin will be able to overcome these challenges and realize its full potential as a global currency.

Chapter 4: Bitcoin's Community and Culture
The Cypherpunk Legacy

The development of Bitcoin was greatly influenced by the cypherpunk movement, a group of individuals interested in cryptography and privacy that emerged in the 1980s. The cypherpunks believed in the power of encryption to protect individual privacy and freedom, and many of their ideas are reflected in the design of Bitcoin.

The cypherpunk movement was a response to the increasing surveillance and control of governments and corporations. In the 1970s, the US government began regulating the use of cryptography as a national security measure, which meant that individuals and businesses could not use strong encryption without government approval. This limited the ability of individuals to communicate privately and securely, and the cypherpunks sought to change this.

One of the key ideas of the cypherpunks was the concept of "cypherpunk remailers", which were designed to allow anonymous communication through email. These remailers used a system of encryption and routing to prevent anyone from tracing the origin of a message. This idea of anonymous communication was later incorporated into Bitcoin through the use of pseudonyms and public keys.

Another key idea of the cypherpunks was the concept of "digital cash". The idea was to create a form of money that could be transferred electronically without the need for a central authority. This idea was realized through the invention of Bitcoin, which uses a decentralized network of nodes to process and validate transactions.

The cypherpunks also believed in the power of cryptography to protect individual privacy and freedom. This is reflected in the design of Bitcoin, which uses cryptographic algorithms to ensure the security and privacy of transactions.

The cypherpunk legacy continues to influence the development of Bitcoin and other cryptocurrencies. Many of the core ideas and values of the cypherpunks, such as privacy, decentralization, and individual freedom, are central to the design and philosophy of Bitcoin. As the use of cryptocurrencies continues to grow, it is likely that the influence of the cypherpunks will continue to be felt for many years to come.

The Bitcoin Community

The Bitcoin community is a decentralized network of individuals, companies, and organizations who use or support the use of Bitcoin. It is a global community that spans across borders and cultures, united by a shared interest in this revolutionary technology.

The community has grown rapidly since the creation of Bitcoin in 2008. In the early days, it was primarily made up of early adopters, libertarians, and computer enthusiasts who were drawn to the idea of a decentralized currency system that operated outside of government control. Over time, the community has expanded to include investors, entrepreneurs, academics, and mainstream users who are interested in the potential benefits of Bitcoin.

One of the defining characteristics of the Bitcoin community is its open and transparent nature. Anyone can participate in the community, and there are no gatekeepers or central authorities. Instead, the community is self-organizing, with individuals and groups coming together to build infrastructure, develop software, and create new use cases for Bitcoin.

There are many ways to get involved in the Bitcoin community, depending on one's interests and skills. For developers, contributing to the open-source Bitcoin software is a popular option. There are also many Bitcoin-related startups and companies that are always looking for talented individuals to join their teams.

The Bitcoin community also has a strong social component, with many online forums, chat rooms, and social media channels dedicated to discussing Bitcoin-related topics. These platforms provide a space for members of the community to share ideas, ask questions, and collaborate on new projects.

One of the key strengths of the Bitcoin community is its resilience. Over the years, Bitcoin has faced many challenges, including regulatory crackdowns, price volatility, and technical difficulties. However, the community has always rallied together to overcome these obstacles and continue building the future of money.

There are many examples of the Bitcoin community coming together to support one another in times of need. For example, in 2014, the Bitcoin community rallied around Mt. Gox users who had lost their funds due to the exchange's collapse. The community created the Bitcoin Foundation's Bitcoin Appeal to provide financial support for those affected by the disaster.

Another notable example of the Bitcoin community's resilience is the ongoing development of the Lightning

Network. The Lightning Network is a second-layer scaling solution that allows for faster and cheaper Bitcoin transactions. Despite facing many technical challenges, the Lightning Network continues to grow and evolve thanks to the efforts of dedicated developers and community members.

Overall, the Bitcoin community is a dynamic and diverse group of individuals and organizations united by a shared vision for the future of money. Despite facing many challenges, the community has continued to grow and innovate, pushing the boundaries of what is possible with Bitcoin. As Bitcoin continues to evolve and mature, the community will undoubtedly play a critical role in shaping its future.

Satoshi's Vision for Bitcoin's Future

Satoshi Nakamoto, the creator of Bitcoin, is known for his enigmatic personality and secretive identity. Despite disappearing from the public eye in 2011, his vision for Bitcoin's future still resonates with many in the community.

Satoshi's initial white paper laid out his vision for a peer-to-peer electronic cash system that would enable individuals to transact without the need for intermediaries like banks or governments. His vision was grounded in the belief that financial privacy is a fundamental right and that individuals should have full control over their money.

In a series of posts on the BitcoinTalk forum, Satoshi elaborated on his vision for Bitcoin's future, touching on various aspects of the technology and its potential uses. Here, we'll examine some of his key ideas.

Decentralization

Satoshi believed that decentralization was critical to Bitcoin's success. He envisioned a network of nodes that would verify and validate transactions, rather than a central authority. This would prevent any single entity from controlling the network and allow Bitcoin to function independently of any government or financial institution.

In one forum post, Satoshi wrote: "The root problem with conventional currency is all the trust that's required to make it work. The central bank must be trusted not to debase the currency, but the history of fiat currencies is full of breaches of that trust."

Satoshi's solution was a decentralized system that relied on cryptography and consensus to secure the network. He saw this as the key innovation of Bitcoin and believed it would fundamentally change the way people think about money.

Scalability

Another area where Satoshi had a clear vision was scalability. He recognized early on that for Bitcoin to become a global currency, it needed to be able to process a large number of transactions quickly and efficiently.

In a post on the BitcoinTalk forum, Satoshi wrote: "We need a system where the workload is spread out evenly among the nodes. We don't want people to have to have large server farms to mine because that will only result in centralization."

To address this, Satoshi proposed a solution called the "block size limit," which limited the size of each block of transactions on the Bitcoin blockchain. This was intended to prevent the blockchain from becoming too large and unwieldy, while still allowing for a high volume of transactions.

Privacy

Satoshi also believed in the importance of financial privacy. He saw Bitcoin as a way for individuals to transact without the need for third-party intermediaries who could potentially compromise their financial privacy.

In a forum post, Satoshi wrote: "The traditional banking model achieves a level of privacy by limiting access to information to the parties involved and the trusted third party. The necessity to announce all transactions publicly precludes this method, but privacy can still be maintained by breaking the flow of information in another place: by keeping public keys anonymous."

This led to the development of the pseudonymous nature of Bitcoin transactions, where users are identified by a public key rather than their real name.

Openness

Finally, Satoshi believed in the importance of openness and transparency in the development of Bitcoin. He recognized that the success of the project relied on the contributions of a large and diverse community of developers, users, and enthusiasts.

In a post on the BitcoinTalk forum, Satoshi wrote: "Bitcoin is open source... anyone can review the code. I made it open source because I know that the strength of Bitcoin lies in its openness. Anyone can improve on the code, just like anyone can improve on Wikipedia."

This openness and transparency have been key to Bitcoin's success. The community has been able to identify and fix bugs and security vulnerabilities, as well as propose and implement new features and upgrades.

Conclusion

Although Satoshi Nakamoto disappeared from the public eye over a decade ago, his vision for Bitcoin's future remains influential in the community. His belief in decentralization, privacy, and freedom from government control has inspired countless individuals and organizations to embrace the revolutionary potential of cryptocurrency. Satoshi's legacy extends far beyond the development of a digital currency; he has catalyzed a movement of individuals committed to challenging the status quo and creating a more equitable and transparent financial system.

As the world continues to grapple with issues of economic inequality, political instability, and technological disruption, the significance of Satoshi's contributions to the world of cryptocurrency cannot be overstated. The development of Bitcoin and the subsequent growth of the cryptocurrency industry has spurred innovation and experimentation in fields as diverse as finance, law, and computer science.

Despite the challenges and controversies that have arisen around Bitcoin over the years, it remains a powerful symbol of hope and possibility for those who believe in the transformative potential of technology. As the story of Satoshi Nakamoto continues to unfold, it will undoubtedly inspire and influence future generations of entrepreneurs, technologists, and activists seeking to create a better world.

Chapter 5: Legal and Regulatory Challenges
Bitcoin and the Law

Bitcoin, as a decentralized digital currency, operates outside of the traditional financial system and presents a unique challenge for legal and regulatory frameworks around the world. While some countries have embraced Bitcoin and other cryptocurrencies, others have been more skeptical, and the legal status of Bitcoin varies significantly between jurisdictions.

One of the main legal challenges posed by Bitcoin is its potential for use in illegal activities such as money laundering, drug trafficking, and terrorism financing. While these concerns are not unique to Bitcoin, its decentralized nature and pseudonymous transactions make it more difficult for law enforcement to track and identify criminal activities.

Many countries have responded to these concerns by implementing regulations that require Bitcoin exchanges and other cryptocurrency businesses to follow Know Your Customer (KYC) and Anti-Money Laundering (AML) procedures. These regulations are designed to prevent criminals from using Bitcoin to carry out illegal activities and to ensure that Bitcoin transactions are transparent and traceable.

However, the decentralized nature of Bitcoin also means that it is difficult for governments to enforce these regulations, and there are concerns that excessive regulation could stifle innovation in the cryptocurrency industry. In some countries, such as China, the government has even banned Bitcoin and other cryptocurrencies altogether, citing concerns over financial stability and the potential for fraud.

Another legal challenge for Bitcoin is its treatment under tax laws. While some countries, such as the United States, have classified Bitcoin as property for tax purposes, others have yet to establish a clear legal framework for the taxation of cryptocurrencies. This lack of clarity has led to confusion and uncertainty for Bitcoin users and businesses.

Overall, the legal and regulatory challenges facing Bitcoin are complex and multifaceted. While there is a need to address concerns around illegal activities and financial stability, excessive regulation could stifle innovation in the cryptocurrency industry. Finding a balance between these competing interests will be key to the long-term success of Bitcoin and other cryptocurrencies.

Government Responses to Bitcoin

Introduction: Bitcoin is a decentralized digital currency that operates without the need for intermediaries, such as banks or government institutions. As a result, governments around the world have struggled to develop appropriate regulatory frameworks to govern the use of Bitcoin. Some governments have been more proactive than others, while others have banned Bitcoin outright. This chapter will explore the different responses of governments to the rise of Bitcoin.

Government Responses to Bitcoin: The response of governments to Bitcoin has varied widely. In some countries, governments have taken a proactive approach to regulating Bitcoin, while in others, the government has banned its use outright. The United States has taken a moderate approach to Bitcoin, with a mix of regulation and enforcement. In 2013, the US Treasury Department's Financial Crimes Enforcement Network (FinCEN) issued guidance that classified Bitcoin as a type of currency and mandated that Bitcoin exchanges comply with anti-money laundering (AML) and know-your-customer (KYC) regulations. In 2015, the US Commodity Futures Trading Commission (CFTC) also classified Bitcoin as a commodity subject to regulation.

The European Union has also been proactive in its approach to regulating Bitcoin. In 2016, the European Parliament passed a directive requiring virtual currency exchanges and wallet providers to register with the appropriate regulatory authorities and comply with AML and KYC regulations. Additionally, the European Central Bank has issued statements warning consumers of the risks associated with virtual currencies.

Other countries, however, have taken a much more hostile approach to Bitcoin. In 2017, China banned initial coin offerings (ICOs), which are a form of crowdfunding that use cryptocurrencies, and shut down Bitcoin exchanges in the country. Similarly, in 2018, the Indian government banned banks from dealing with cryptocurrency exchanges and individuals trading cryptocurrencies. The Russian government has also taken a cautious approach to Bitcoin, with the central bank warning that virtual currencies pose significant risks to consumers.

Conclusion: The response of governments to Bitcoin has been varied and often cautious. While some countries have taken a proactive approach to regulating Bitcoin, others have banned its use outright. However, as Bitcoin becomes increasingly mainstream, governments around the world will need to develop appropriate regulatory frameworks that balance the benefits of innovation with the need to protect consumers and maintain financial stability. It is likely that the regulatory landscape for Bitcoin will continue to evolve in the years ahead as governments grapple with the challenges posed by this new technology.

The Future of Bitcoin Regulation

The regulation of Bitcoin has been a contentious issue since its inception, and it continues to evolve as governments and regulatory bodies attempt to grapple with the technology's impact on traditional financial systems. The future of Bitcoin regulation is a topic of much debate, with some advocating for a laissez-faire approach and others calling for stricter oversight.

One of the key challenges in regulating Bitcoin is determining which agency or agencies should be responsible for overseeing the technology. In the United States, for example, Bitcoin is subject to oversight by several regulatory bodies, including the Financial Crimes Enforcement Network (FinCEN), the Securities and Exchange Commission (SEC), and the Commodity Futures Trading Commission (CFTC). This fragmented approach has led to confusion and uncertainty among market participants and has made it difficult for businesses operating in the space to comply with regulations.

Another challenge is the global nature of Bitcoin. Unlike traditional financial systems, which are largely confined to national borders, Bitcoin is a borderless technology that can be used by anyone with an internet connection. This has made it difficult for governments to enforce regulations and has led to concerns about the use of Bitcoin for illicit activities such as money laundering and terrorism financing.

Despite these challenges, many in the Bitcoin community believe that regulation is necessary to bring legitimacy to the technology and to protect consumers from fraud and abuse. Some have even called for the creation of a new regulatory framework specifically designed for cryptocurrencies.

One potential model for such a framework is the New York BitLicense, which was introduced in 2015 by the New York State Department of Financial Services (NYDFS). The BitLicense requires companies operating in the cryptocurrency space to obtain a license and comply with a range of regulatory requirements, including anti-money laundering (AML) and know-your-customer (KYC) rules.

While the BitLicense has been criticized by some in the Bitcoin community for being too onerous, others see it as a step in the right direction. Some have even called for other states and countries to adopt similar frameworks in order to create a more consistent regulatory environment for cryptocurrencies.

Ultimately, the future of Bitcoin regulation is likely to be shaped by a range of factors, including the actions of governments and regulatory bodies, the attitudes of market participants, and the evolution of the technology itself. While it is impossible to predict exactly how regulation will evolve, it is clear that the issue will continue to be a topic of much debate and discussion in the years to come.

Chapter 6: Satoshi's Legacy
The Ongoing Impact of Bitcoin

Since the launch of Bitcoin in 2009, it has grown to become the most widely adopted cryptocurrency in the world. Bitcoin's decentralized architecture and open-source codebase have made it a favorite of libertarians, anarchists, and other privacy advocates. But Bitcoin has also become a mainstream investment option, with large institutional investors and corporations buying up significant amounts of Bitcoin.

The impact of Bitcoin has been felt across multiple industries and sectors, from finance and technology to gaming and e-commerce. Bitcoin's ability to facilitate fast and low-cost cross-border transactions has made it a popular choice for international money transfers and remittances. Bitcoin's digital nature has also made it a preferred medium of exchange for online transactions and purchases, particularly in the gaming and e-commerce sectors.

Bitcoin's impact on the financial industry has been particularly significant. Traditional financial institutions have been forced to adapt to the rise of Bitcoin and other cryptocurrencies, with many banks and financial institutions exploring ways to incorporate blockchain technology into their operations. The use of blockchain technology for secure and efficient record-keeping has also been explored by governments and businesses.

Beyond its practical applications, Bitcoin has also had a significant cultural impact. Its decentralized and permissionless nature has attracted a community of passionate supporters who see it as a tool for promoting individual liberty and autonomy. Bitcoin's supporters have created a unique subculture, complete with its own jargon, memes, and rituals.

Despite its ongoing impact, the future of Bitcoin remains uncertain. While Bitcoin has proven itself to be resilient in the face of regulatory and legal challenges, there are still many obstacles that it will need to overcome if it is to become a truly mainstream currency. These obstacles include regulatory uncertainty, technological limitations, and ongoing concerns around security and privacy.

Bitcoin's ongoing impact is also linked to the legacy of its mysterious creator, Satoshi Nakamoto. Satoshi's decision to remain anonymous has only added to the allure and mystique surrounding Bitcoin. Satoshi's vision for Bitcoin's future continues to shape the development of the cryptocurrency, and his influence can be seen in everything from the ongoing debates around scaling and governance to the development of new features and applications.

In conclusion, the ongoing impact of Bitcoin is hard to overstate. Bitcoin has become a cultural, economic, and technological force that shows no signs of slowing down. Its impact will continue to be felt across multiple industries and sectors for years to come, and its legacy will continue to inspire new innovations and developments in the cryptocurrency space.

Satoshi's Role in the Crypto Revolution

Satoshi Nakamoto's contribution to the world of cryptocurrency extends beyond the creation of Bitcoin. His work sparked a revolution in the financial world, inspiring the development of new decentralized technologies, and giving rise to an entirely new industry.

The release of the Bitcoin whitepaper in 2008 introduced a new concept of digital currency, which operates without the need for intermediaries like banks or governments. This revolutionary idea has inspired the development of numerous cryptocurrencies, including Ethereum, Litecoin, and Dogecoin. The creation of these currencies has helped to establish a thriving ecosystem of decentralized finance, allowing for more accessible, transparent, and secure transactions worldwide.

Moreover, Satoshi's decision to remain anonymous and decentralize the development process has influenced the crypto community's values of privacy, decentralization, and transparency. Bitcoin's open-source code has enabled a network of developers worldwide to collaborate and create new projects that advance the industry's goals.

Satoshi's influence extends beyond cryptocurrency into the world of blockchain technology. Bitcoin's blockchain technology has inspired new applications in various industries, including supply chain management, voting systems, and identity verification.

Satoshi's work has also inspired a new generation of entrepreneurs and developers to challenge traditional financial institutions and create decentralized technologies that can help empower individuals worldwide. The emergence of these projects has led to a democratization of finance, where anyone can participate in the global economy without needing to rely on centralized institutions.

In conclusion, Satoshi Nakamoto's impact on the crypto industry and beyond cannot be overstated. His vision for a decentralized financial system has led to the development of a thriving ecosystem of cryptocurrencies and blockchain technologies, with the potential to transform industries worldwide. Satoshi's legacy will continue to inspire innovation and challenge traditional financial institutions for years to come.

Satoshi's Legacy for Future Generations

Satoshi Nakamoto's legacy extends far beyond the creation of Bitcoin. He has become a symbol of innovation and the potential of technology to disrupt traditional industries. As more people learn about Bitcoin and its impact on society, Satoshi's legacy will continue to grow. Here are some of the ways that Satoshi's legacy is shaping the future:

1. Innovation and Disruption: Satoshi's vision of a decentralized, peer-to-peer payment system has inspired countless entrepreneurs and developers to explore new ways of using blockchain technology. Bitcoin has already disrupted the traditional banking industry and is now being used in a variety of industries, from healthcare to real estate. As new use cases for blockchain technology are discovered, Satoshi's legacy will continue to inspire innovation and disruption.

2. Financial Inclusion: Satoshi's vision of a financial system that is accessible to everyone, regardless of their geographic location or socioeconomic status, is still being realized today. Bitcoin has the potential to provide financial services to the unbanked and underbanked populations of the world. By eliminating the need for traditional banking infrastructure, Bitcoin can reduce the cost of financial services and make them more widely available.

3. Privacy and Security: Satoshi's focus on privacy and security in the Bitcoin protocol has set a new standard for digital transactions. As more people become aware of the importance of online privacy and the risks of centralized control, Satoshi's legacy will inspire further development of secure and private technologies.

4. Community and Collaboration: Satoshi's creation of an open-source, decentralized platform has fostered a global community of developers and users who are working together to improve the Bitcoin protocol. This community has inspired other open-source projects and has become a model for collaboration in the tech industry.

5. Intellectual Property: Satoshi's decision to remain anonymous and release the Bitcoin code as open source has raised important questions about intellectual property and the role of patents in the tech industry. Satoshi's legacy has helped spark a debate about the value of open-source software and the potential harm that can come from patent trolling and other forms of intellectual property abuse.

In conclusion, Satoshi Nakamoto's legacy extends far beyond the creation of Bitcoin. His vision of a decentralized, peer-to-peer payment system has inspired innovation, financial inclusion, privacy and security, community and collaboration, and a new approach to intellectual property in the tech industry. As the world continues to grapple with the challenges and opportunities of blockchain technology, Satoshi's legacy will continue to shape the future of innovation and disruption.

Chapter 7: The Future of Cryptocurrency
The Evolution of Cryptocurrency

The rise of Bitcoin has paved the way for the development of other cryptocurrencies, and the future of the digital currency landscape is constantly evolving. In this section, we will explore the evolution of cryptocurrencies, from the first altcoins to the current state of the market, and what the future might hold.

The first altcoin, Namecoin, was launched in 2011. It aimed to provide a decentralized domain name system (DNS), allowing users to register domains without the need for a centralized authority. While Namecoin never gained widespread adoption, it paved the way for the development of other altcoins, each with their own unique features and use cases.

Litecoin was the next significant altcoin, launched in 2011 by Charlie Lee. It was designed to be faster and more efficient than Bitcoin, with a four times faster block time and a different hashing algorithm. Litecoin gained popularity as a "silver to Bitcoin's gold" and has remained a popular cryptocurrency to this day.

Ethereum, launched in 2015, is another significant milestone in the evolution of cryptocurrencies. It introduced the concept of smart contracts, allowing developers to build decentralized applications (dApps) on top of its blockchain. This feature enabled the development of new use cases for blockchain technology beyond simple peer-to-peer transactions.

Other significant cryptocurrencies include Ripple, which aimed to revolutionize the banking industry with its fast and cheap cross-border payment system, and Bitcoin Cash, a fork of Bitcoin designed to improve transaction speed and scalability.

Currently, the cryptocurrency market is dominated by Bitcoin, with a market capitalization of over $1 trillion. However, there are thousands of other cryptocurrencies in existence, each with their own unique features and use cases. Some, like Ethereum and Binance Coin, have established themselves as major players in the market, while others remain niche cryptocurrencies with smaller communities.

Looking to the future, there are several trends that could shape the evolution of cryptocurrencies. One is the development of central bank digital currencies (CBDCs), which are digital versions of traditional fiat currencies. Several central banks, including the People's Bank of China and the European Central Bank, are currently exploring CBDCs, which could further legitimize the use of digital currencies and lead to increased adoption.

Another trend is the growth of decentralized finance (DeFi) applications, which are built on top of blockchain technology and aim to replace traditional financial intermediaries with decentralized protocols. DeFi has seen explosive growth in recent years, with the total value locked in DeFi protocols reaching over $100 billion in 2021. As the DeFi ecosystem continues to grow and mature, it could become a significant driver of demand for cryptocurrencies.

Finally, the development of new use cases for cryptocurrencies, such as non-fungible tokens (NFTs) and decentralized social media platforms, could also play a significant role in the future of cryptocurrencies.

In conclusion, the evolution of cryptocurrencies has been rapid and constantly evolving since the launch of Bitcoin in 2009. While Bitcoin remains the dominant cryptocurrency, other altcoins and blockchain-based applications have emerged, each with their own unique features and use cases. Looking to the future, the growth of CBDCs, DeFi, and new use cases could shape the future of the cryptocurrency landscape.

Potential for Decentralization

Decentralization is one of the key principles that underpins the creation of cryptocurrencies, and it is also one of the key factors that sets them apart from traditional forms of currency. Unlike fiat currency, which is centralized and controlled by governments or central banks, cryptocurrencies are designed to operate in a decentralized manner, with no central authority or intermediary overseeing transactions. This decentralization is achieved through the use of blockchain technology, which creates a distributed ledger that is maintained by a network of users, rather than a single central authority.

The potential for decentralization is one of the most exciting aspects of cryptocurrency, and it has the potential to transform a wide range of industries and applications. By eliminating the need for intermediaries and centralized authorities, cryptocurrencies can help to reduce transaction costs, increase transparency and security, and enable greater innovation and collaboration.

One of the key areas where the potential for decentralization is being explored is in the financial sector. Cryptocurrencies have already disrupted traditional finance to a certain extent, with many people now using them as an alternative to fiat currencies or as a store of value. However, there is still a long way to go in terms of achieving true decentralization in finance. Many financial services and products are still heavily reliant on centralized intermediaries, such as banks, stock exchanges, and clearing houses.

Decentralized finance, or DeFi, is a movement that seeks to address these issues by creating a more open and decentralized financial system. DeFi projects use blockchain technology to create new financial products and services that are accessible to anyone with an internet connection, rather than being restricted to a select group of intermediaries. This includes things like peer-to-peer lending, decentralized exchanges, and automated market makers.

Another area where decentralization has the potential to make a significant impact is in the area of governance. Traditional forms of governance are often centralized and hierarchical, with power concentrated in the hands of a small group of individuals or organizations. This can lead to corruption, inefficiency, and a lack of transparency.

Blockchain technology has the potential to enable new forms of decentralized governance, where decisions are made through a transparent and decentralized process. This can include things like blockchain-based voting systems, decentralized autonomous organizations (DAOs), and other forms of decentralized decision-making.

Overall, the potential for decentralization is one of the most exciting aspects of the cryptocurrency revolution. While there are still many challenges to overcome, the potential for a more open, transparent, and decentralized world is truly revolutionary. As the technology continues to evolve and mature, it is likely that we will see even more innovative and exciting applications of blockchain technology in the years to come.

The Future of Money

The concept of money has evolved over time, from bartering goods to using precious metals, paper currency, and digital transactions. Cryptocurrency, particularly Bitcoin, has introduced a new form of money that challenges the traditional monetary system. In this section, we will discuss the potential future of money and how cryptocurrency may play a role in shaping it.

One of the most significant benefits of cryptocurrency is its potential to increase financial inclusion. Traditional banking systems can be exclusive, particularly for people living in underdeveloped countries or those without access to financial services. Cryptocurrency allows anyone with an internet connection to participate in the financial system, regardless of their location or socioeconomic status. This has the potential to provide financial empowerment to millions of people worldwide.

Another potential benefit of cryptocurrency is its potential to increase transparency and reduce corruption. Blockchain technology, the underlying technology behind cryptocurrency, allows for secure and transparent record-keeping. This means that transactions can be tracked, verified, and validated in real-time, increasing accountability and reducing the likelihood of fraud.

Cryptocurrency also has the potential to reduce transaction fees and increase transaction speed. Traditional financial institutions charge fees for transactions, particularly for cross-border payments. Cryptocurrency transactions, on the other hand, can be processed quickly and at a fraction of the cost, potentially making it more accessible to people who cannot afford high transaction fees.

However, there are also potential drawbacks to cryptocurrency's role in the future of money. One of the most significant concerns is its volatility. Cryptocurrencies, particularly Bitcoin, are known for their extreme price fluctuations, which can make them difficult to use as a reliable store of value. This has the potential to discourage widespread adoption and use.

Another concern is the lack of regulation and oversight. The decentralized nature of cryptocurrency makes it challenging to regulate and control, which can create opportunities for illicit activities, such as money laundering and terrorism financing. This has led to calls for increased regulation and oversight to ensure that cryptocurrency is not used for nefarious purposes.

In conclusion, the future of money is uncertain, but cryptocurrency has the potential to play a significant role in shaping it. Its potential benefits, such as financial inclusion, transparency, and reduced transaction fees, are compelling. However, its volatility and lack of regulation and oversight are significant concerns that must be addressed for it to gain widespread adoption and use. As cryptocurrency continues to evolve and mature, it will be fascinating to see how it impacts the future of money.

Conclusion

Satoshi's Contributions to the World

Satoshi Nakamoto's invention of Bitcoin has had a significant impact on the world, both in terms of the technology itself and the ideas that it represents. This chapter will explore Satoshi's contributions to the world, including the ways in which his invention has changed the way we think about money, trust, and decentralization.

One of Satoshi's most significant contributions to the world is the creation of a decentralized digital currency that can be used without the need for intermediaries such as banks. Before Bitcoin, there was no way to transfer value over the internet without relying on a trusted third party to verify the transaction. Satoshi's invention of the blockchain technology solved this problem by creating a trustless system in which users could transact with each other directly, without the need for a trusted intermediary.

Another contribution that Satoshi made to the world was the idea of a decentralized network of nodes that work together to validate transactions and maintain the integrity of the blockchain. This network of nodes allows for a high degree of security and trust in the system, as no single entity can control the entire network.

Satoshi's vision for a decentralized currency has also influenced the way we think about money and trust. Before Bitcoin, there was a widespread belief that central banks and governments were necessary to ensure the stability and security of a currency. Satoshi's invention of Bitcoin challenged this belief by showing that it was possible to create a secure and stable currency without the need for a central authority.

Satoshi's contributions to the world have also inspired a new generation of developers and entrepreneurs to create innovative solutions using blockchain technology. The success of Bitcoin has led to the creation of thousands of new cryptocurrencies, as well as a range of other applications that use blockchain technology, such as smart contracts, decentralized exchanges, and voting systems.

In addition to his contributions to technology, Satoshi has also inspired a movement of people who believe in the principles of decentralization and freedom. The cypherpunk movement, which Satoshi was a part of, has long advocated for the use of cryptography and other technologies to protect privacy and empower individuals. Satoshi's invention of Bitcoin has helped to bring these ideas to a wider audience, and has inspired many people to become involved in the movement.

In conclusion, Satoshi Nakamoto's contributions to the world are significant and far-reaching. His invention of Bitcoin has changed the way we think about money, trust, and decentralization, and has inspired a new generation of developers and entrepreneurs to create innovative solutions using blockchain technology. His vision for a decentralized currency has challenged the status quo and inspired a movement of people who believe in the principles of freedom and empowerment. Satoshi's legacy will continue to inspire and shape the future of technology and society for many years to come.

Continuing Legacy of Bitcoin

Bitcoin has come a long way since its inception over a decade ago, and its impact on the world has been significant. As the world's first decentralized digital currency, Bitcoin has introduced a new paradigm for money and finance, with the potential to disrupt traditional financial institutions and transform the way we conduct transactions.

Despite its anonymous creator, Satoshi Nakamoto, disappearing from the public eye, his legacy lives on in the Bitcoin community. His vision for a decentralized currency and his innovative approach to solving the double-spending problem have inspired countless others to pursue the development and advancement of blockchain technology.

As Bitcoin continues to evolve, its potential applications are expanding beyond just a digital currency. Smart contracts, decentralized finance, and non-fungible tokens (NFTs) are just a few examples of how blockchain technology is being used to create new solutions to age-old problems.

The continuing legacy of Bitcoin is not just limited to the technology itself, but also to the community that has formed around it. The open-source nature of Bitcoin has allowed for anyone with an internet connection to participate in its development and use. This has led to a diverse and passionate community, with members from all around the world working together to push the boundaries of what is possible with blockchain technology.

One of the most significant contributions of Bitcoin to the world is the idea of decentralization. By removing intermediaries from financial transactions, Bitcoin has paved the way for a more peer-to-peer economy. This has the potential to create more opportunities for people who are underserved by traditional financial institutions, as well as reducing the power of centralized institutions over the global financial system.

Furthermore, Bitcoin's success has inspired the development of countless other cryptocurrencies, each with their own unique properties and potential use cases. The proliferation of these cryptocurrencies has created a more competitive market, driving innovation and improvements in the technology.

In conclusion, the legacy of Bitcoin is far-reaching and multifaceted. Satoshi Nakamoto's contributions to the world extend beyond just the development of the technology itself. His creation of Bitcoin has inspired a movement towards decentralization, created a vibrant community of developers and enthusiasts, and paved the way for new and innovative applications of blockchain technology. As the world continues to evolve, it is clear that the legacy of Bitcoin will continue to play an important role in shaping the future of finance and technology.

The Importance of Satoshi's Story

The story of Satoshi Nakamoto and the creation of Bitcoin has had an enormous impact on the world. Satoshi's vision for a decentralized, digital currency has inspired a global community and revolutionized the way we think about money and trust. But beyond the technical innovations and economic implications, Satoshi's story is important for what it tells us about the human experience.

Satoshi's story is a reminder of the power of anonymity and the importance of privacy in a world where our personal information is constantly under threat. It's a story of a lone individual taking on an entrenched system and succeeding through sheer force of will and ingenuity. It's a story of hope and possibility, of what can be achieved when we dare to dream big and challenge the status quo.

But perhaps most importantly, Satoshi's story is a reminder of the power of community and collaboration. Bitcoin was not created in a vacuum - it was the result of a collective effort by a diverse group of individuals who shared a common vision. Satoshi's decision to release the code as open-source software was a critical factor in Bitcoin's success, as it allowed others to contribute to the project and build on its foundation.

The Bitcoin community that has emerged in the years since the creation of Bitcoin is a testament to the enduring power of Satoshi's vision. It is a vibrant and diverse community that spans the globe, united by a shared belief in the potential of decentralized, trustless systems. The community has faced numerous challenges over the years, from government crackdowns to internal debates over the direction of the project. But through it all, the community has remained committed to the principles that Satoshi laid out in the original Bitcoin whitepaper.

Satoshi's story is also a cautionary tale about the potential pitfalls of success. As Bitcoin has grown in popularity and value, it has attracted the attention of governments and corporations around the world. Some have embraced Bitcoin as a disruptive force that has the potential to transform the financial system, while others have viewed it as a threat to their power and control. The legal and regulatory challenges facing Bitcoin are complex and ever-changing, and it is unclear what the future holds for the technology.

Despite these challenges, the legacy of Satoshi and Bitcoin will continue to shape the world in profound ways. The principles of decentralization, transparency, and trustlessness that underpin the technology have the potential to transform not just the financial system, but the way we think about governance, identity, and power. The story of Satoshi and Bitcoin is a reminder that even the most revolutionary ideas can take root and flourish, given the right conditions and a committed community.

In the end, the importance of Satoshi's story lies not just in the creation of a new technology, but in the way it has sparked a global conversation about the future of money and trust. Satoshi's vision has inspired countless individuals to explore the potential of decentralized systems, and has given rise to a movement that is pushing the boundaries of what is possible. As we look to the future, we can be certain that the story of Satoshi and Bitcoin will continue to inspire and guide us, as we work to create a more open, transparent, and equitable world.

THE END

Key Terms and Definitions

To help you better understand the language and concepts related to aging and older adults, below you will find a list of key terms and their definitions.

1. Satoshi Nakamoto: A pseudonym used by the unknown person or group of people who created and initially authored the original Bitcoin white paper and implemented the first Bitcoin software.

2. Bitcoin: A decentralized digital currency that uses cryptography for security and operates on a peer-to-peer network without the need for intermediaries such as banks or governments.

3. Blockchain: A decentralized, distributed ledger that records transactions across a network of computers, making it immutable and tamper-resistant.

4. Cryptocurrency: A digital or virtual currency that uses cryptography for security and operates on a decentralized network.

5. Mining: The process of verifying and recording transactions on a blockchain network by solving complex mathematical equations using computing power.

6. Wallet: A digital storage device that holds public and private keys used to access and manage cryptocurrency.

7. Decentralization: A system that operates on a distributed network with no central authority or control.

8. Cypherpunk: A movement advocating the use of strong cryptography and privacy-enhancing technologies as a means to achieve social and political change.

9. Regulation: Rules and guidelines established by governments or regulatory bodies to control and supervise the use and exchange of cryptocurrencies.

10. Adoption: The process of individuals, businesses, and institutions accepting and integrating cryptocurrencies into their daily operations and transactions.

Supporting Materials

Introduction:

- Bitcoin.org. (2022). Bitcoin: A Peer-to-Peer Electronic Cash System. https://bitcoin.org/bitcoin.pdf

Chapter 1: The Development of Bitcoin:

- Nakamoto, S. (2008). Bitcoin: A Peer-to-Peer Electronic Cash System. https://bitcoin.org/bitcoin.pdf

- Popper, N. (2015). Digital Gold: Bitcoin and the Inside Story of the Misfits and Millionaires Trying to Reinvent Money. Harper.

Chapter 2: Satoshi's Personal Life:

- Davis, J. (2011). The Crypto-Currency: Bitcoin and its mysterious inventor. The New Yorker. https://www.newyorker.com/magazine/2011/10/10/the-crypto-currency

- Penenberg, A. L. (2018). The Mysterious Disappearance of Satoshi Nakamoto, Founder of Bitcoin. Wired. https://www.wired.com/story/the-mysterious-disappearance-of-satoshi-nakamoto/

Chapter 3: The Impact of Bitcoin on the World:

- Antonopoulos, A. M. (2014). Mastering Bitcoin: Unlocking Digital Cryptocurrencies. O'Reilly Media.

- Vigna, P., & Casey, M. J. (2015). The Age of Cryptocurrency: How Bitcoin and Digital Money are Challenging the Global Economic Order. St. Martin's Press.

Chapter 4: Bitcoin's Community and Culture:

- Swan, M. (2015). Blockchain: Blueprint for a New Economy. O'Reilly Media.

- Tapscott, D., & Tapscott, A. (2016). Blockchain Revolution: How the Technology Behind Bitcoin Is Changing Money, Business, and the World. Penguin.

Chapter 5: Legal and Regulatory Challenges:

- Athey, S., & Parashkevov, I. (2018). Bitcoin and Cryptocurrency Technologies: A Comprehensive Introduction. Princeton University Press.

- Yermack, D. (2015). Is Bitcoin a Real Currency? An Economic Appraisal. NBER Working Paper No. 19747. https://www.nber.org/papers/w19747.pdf

Chapter 6: Satoshi's Legacy:

- Casey, M. J. (2021). The Cryptocurrency Revolution: The Future of Money? Yale University Press.

- Popper, N. (2019). Digital Cash: The Unknown History of the Anarchists, Technologists, and Utopians Who Created Cryptocurrency. Harper.

Chapter 7: The Future of Cryptocurrency:

- Buterin, V. (2014). A Next-Generation Smart Contract and Decentralized Application Platform. https://ethereum.org/en/whitepaper/

- Tschorsch, F., & Scheuermann, B. (2016). Bitcoin and Beyond: A Technical Survey on Decentralized Digital Currencies. IEEE Communications Surveys & Tutorials, 18(3), 2084-2123.

Conclusion:

- Nakamoto, S. (2008). Bitcoin: A Peer-to-Peer Electronic Cash System. https://bitcoin.org/bitcoin.pdf

- Swan, M. (2015). Blockchain: Blueprint for a New Economy. O'Reilly Media.